GW00457564

DON'T GIVE A FOX!

www.booksbyboxer.com

Bee Three Publishing is an imprint of Books By Boxer
Published by
Books By Boxer, Leeds, LS13 4BS UK
Books by Boxer (EU), Dublin D02 P593 IRELAND
© Books By Boxer 2023
All Rights Reserved
MADE IN CHINA
ISBN: 9781915410108

This book is produced from responsibly sourced paper to ensure forest management

"All our dreams can come true,
if we have the courage
to pursue them."

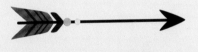

WALT DISNEY

Get Inspired

Bring inspiration to your life
by taking a walk and exploring
somewhere new. It will give you
a sense of adventure and might
even influence new ideas!

PAWS AND BREATHE!

Celebrate Small Things

Reward yourself for the little wins
in life, such as meeting a deadline
or acing a new recipe, as well as
the big ones - to encourage you to
keep on going!

"Everything you can
imagine is real."

PABLO PICASSO

"Don't be afraid to give up the good to go for the great."

JOHN D. ROCKEFELLER

"The secret of getting ahead is getting started."

MARK TWAIN

"Nothing is impossible.
The word itself says
I'm possible!"

AUDREY HEPBURN

"One day or day one.
You decide."

UNKNOWN

Stop Comparing Yourself To Others
Focus On Being Yourself
There are no deadlines in life,
only opportunities!

THINK OUTSIDE THE FOX!

"I'd rather regret the things I've done than regret the things I haven't done."

LUCILLE BALL

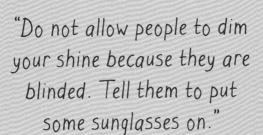

"Do not allow people to dim your shine because they are blinded. Tell them to put some sunglasses on."

LADY GAGA

"Don't settle for average.
Bring your best to the moment.
Then, whether it fails or
succeeds, at least you know
you gave all you had."

ANGELA BASSETT

WHERE DO VIXENS
KEEP THEIR MONEY?

IN THEIR FURSE.

"The only one who can tell you
"you can't win" is you and you
don't have to listen."

JESSICA ENNIS-HILL

"If you can't yet do great things, do small things in a great way."

NAPOLEON HILL

Stay Positive

Banish negative thoughts and ask yourself 'What is good about this situation?' Changing your attitude and focusing on the positives will help you stay inspired!

"Every strike brings me closer to the next home run."

BABE RUTH

Practice Gratitude!

It's much easier to stay motivated when you take a step back and feel appreciation for yourself and your surroundings. Start by writing down three things you're grateful for - these could be as simple as a good cup of coffee that morning, or your dog!

"Be miserable. Or motivate yourself. Whatever has to be done, it's always your choice."

WAYNE DYER

Be Kind To Yourself

Don't beat yourself up over mistakes, and don't say something to yourself if you wouldn't say it to another person!

"People say nothing is
impossible, but I do
nothing every day."

WINNIE THE POOH

"You cannot plow a field by turning it over in your mind. To begin, begin."

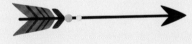

GORDON B. HINCKLEY

"Courage doesn't always roar.
Sometimes courage is a quiet
voice at the end of the day saying,
"I will try again tomorrow.""

MARY ANNE RADMACHER

I'M FUR-BULOUS!

"One of the differences between some successful and unsuccessful people is that one group is full of doers, while the other is full of wishers."

EDMOND MBIAKA

"The elevator to success is out
of order. You'll have to use the
stairs, one step at a time."

JOE GIRARD

Ask Yourself Why

Take 5 minutes out of your day and write down the reasons you want to achieve something as a reminder not to give up!

"The biggest adventure you can
ever take is to live the life
of your dreams."

OPRAH WINFREY

"I can't tell you how many times I've been given a no. Only to find that a better, brighter, bigger yes was right around the corner."

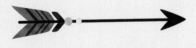

ARLAN HAMILTON

Make It A Habit

If you stay consistent and regularly complete the same action over time, this will become a natural habit and easy to incorporate into your every day - even on days when your motivation is running low!

"Get busy living or get busy dying."

ANDY DUFRESNE
(THE SHAWSHANK REDEMPTION)

Be Patient
You're not always going
to get it right first time; you may
miss a day or mess up - that's okay!
Forgive yourself and don't let it stop
you from trying again tomorrow.

"Do today what others won't
and achieve tomorrow
what others can't."

JERRY RICE

"Champions keep playing until they get it right."

BILLIE JEAN KING

BRIGHT EYED AND
BUSHY TAILED

"I will go anywhere as long as it is forward."

DAVID LIVINGSTON

Take Small Steps

Rome wasn't built in a day!
Don't overwhelm yourself with
a big job list - take small steps
and focus on one thing at a
time - you'll soon have
a city of success!

Visualise Your Journey

Collect pictures and words that represent your vision for what you want to achieve, and present them on a board. This will help you have a clear vision of what to do next!

OUTFOX THEM ALL!

"Some people want it to happen,
some wish it would happen,
others make it happen."

MICHAEL JORDAN

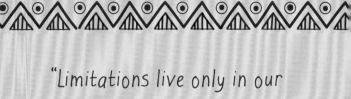

"Limitations live only in our minds. But if we use our imaginations, our possibilities become limitless."

JAMIE PAOLINETTI

Take Notes

If you get a good idea
or see something that interests or
inspires you, note it down! You'll be
surprised how it might help
boost your inspiration!

WHY DID THE FOX CROSS THE ROAD?

TO CHASE THE CHICKEN!

"The best revenge
is massive success."

FRANK SINATRA

"When everything seems to be going against you, remember that the airplane takes off against the wind, not with it."

HENRY FORD

"The most courageous act
is still to think for yourself.
Aloud."

COCO CHANEL

IT CUB BE WORSE!

Love Yourself

Leave little love notes with positive
affirmations around your home on
items like the mirror or your
fridge, to inspire you every time
you look at them!

"You have to have confidence in your ability, and then be tough enough to follow through."

ROSALYNN CARTER

Don't Force It

If you're feeling uninspired or stressed, take a step away from the task and come back to it when you're feeling calm and motivated, to avoid making mistakes!

"If you don't like the road you're walking, start paving another one."

DOLLY PARTON

"I never look back, darling. It
distracts from the now."

EDNA MODE

"The only way of discovering
the limits of the possible is to
venture a little way past them
into the impossible."

ARTHUR C. CLARKE

Keep A Jar

Every time you accomplish something
that makes you proud, write it down
and pop it in a jar. At the end of the
year, you can look back and reflect
on your achievements!

"DON'T GIVE UP, DON'T TAKE ANYTHING PERSONALLY, AND DON'T TAKE NO FOR AN ANSWER."

SOPHIA AMORUSO

Break It Down

Instead of having one massive job on your task list, break it down into multiple smaller tasks - you can watch your progress and ensure you don't miss anything important!

"You'll never get bored when you try something new. There's really no limit to what you can do."

DR. SEUSS

Turn Your Mistakes Into Something Positive

Instead of brooding over mistakes, use them to progress and learn how to avoid it happening again!

"SOMEWHERE, SOMETHING
INCREDIBLE IS WAITING
TO BE KNOWN."

CARL SAGAN

Be you

Don't try to be somebody else
or do things in a way that
doesn't suit you - everyone
does things differently,
and that's okay!

"What you do makes a difference, and you have to decide what kind of difference you want to make."

JANE GOODALL

"I choose to make the rest of
my life the best of my life."

LOUISE HAY

BE A TAIL-BLAZER!

Tutor Your Talent

Not everybody is lucky enough to have a natural-born talent. Where you may lack this, you can instead use persistence and knowledge to get where you want to be!

"People often say that motivation doesn't last. Well, neither does bathing - that's why we recommend it daily."

ZIG ZIGLAR

"Work until your bank account looks like a phone number."

UNKNOWN

"I always wanted to be
somebody, but now I realise I
should have been more specific."

LILY TOMLIN

"Opportunities don't happen,
you create them."

CHRIS GROSSER

Meditate

You don't have to be a pro at
this, just close your eyes,
breathe deeply and clear
your mind of stresses!

"DON'T LET SOMEONE ELSE'S OPINION
OF YOU BECOME YOUR REALITY"

LES BROWN

"If you're not positive energy,
you're negative energy."

MARK CUBAN

Where did the fox go to buy
a new coat?

TO THE RE-TAIL STORE!

Tidy Your Surroundings

A clean desk, fresh plants and a tidy workspace can do wonders to help your mind focus and will let creativity and inspiration thrive with new ideas!

"I am not a product of my circumstances. I am a product of my decisions."

STEPHEN R. COVEY

"The greatest discovery of my generation is that a human being can alter his life by altering his attitudes."

WILLIAM JAMES

Learn Something New

Find a new hobby, study a new language, or even learn fun facts about your favourite TV show or band. Expanding your knowledge will inspire you to learn!

GO FUR IT!

"Success is getting what you want, happiness is wanting what you get."

W. P. KINSELLA

"You learn more from failure
than from success.
Don't let it stop you.
Failure builds character."

UNKNOWN

"We are all different but there's something kind of <u>fantastic</u> about that, isn't there?"

FANTASTIC MR. FOX

"YOU CAN'T HAVE EVERYTHING. WHERE WOULD YOU PUT IT?"

STEVEN WRIGHT

Keep An Open Mind

Don't take things so literally...
think outside the box and turn
something plain and logical into
something creative and wild!

"Take the attitude of a student, never be too big to ask questions, never know too much to learn something new."

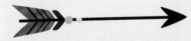

AUGUSTINE OG MANDINO

"I will not lose, for even in defeat, there's a valuable lesson learned, so it evens up for me."

JAY-Z

"SET YOUR GOALS HIGH, AND DON'T STOP TILL YOU GET THERE."

BO JACKSON

Change It Up!

Add your own personal creative
flair into other aspects of
your life, such as changing up
your fashion and decorating
your home to help inspire
creativity wherever you go!

"Life is like riding a bicycle.
To keep your balance you
must keep moving."

ALBERT EINSTEIN

"Think like a queen. A queen is not afraid to fail. Failure is another stepping stone to greatness."

OPRAH WINFREY